# He'll Turn Your Tears to Diamonds

# MY DIAMOND JOURNAL

Dr. Lynda Allen Washington

**He'll Turn Your Tears to Diamonds**
**MY DIAMOND JOURNAL**
Dr. Lynda G. Washington
Author & Evangelist

For Booking Engagements & Book Tour Request:
Dr. Lynda G. Washington
Post Office Box 1671 • Sauk Village, Illinois 60412
(708) 359-2746 • jilotawwm@yahoo.com • www.jilota4law.com

Follow me on Face Book, Twitter, Instagram, LinkedIn, Marco Polo and more! We would love to come teach your group our line dance The LAW!

ISBN: 978-0-9909348-6-8
Printed in the USA.
First printing edition 2018.

PublishAffordably.com
773.783.2981

# My Diamond Journal

## He'll Turn Your Tears To Diamonds

Take this opportunity to reflect on your families last 3 generations of similarities. Traits good or bad passed down. Females or Males it doesn't matter.

During this journey of your journal, focus and you will begin to remember and embrace past, present and future emotions concerning your last 3 generations.

This is your personal **Diamond Journal** where you can capture, your sentiments concerning your family. Do not be afraid to allow your mind to expand, to its fullest capacity, and bring out the treasures of your families experiences. Always remember no matter how painful, bitter, sweet, happy, triumphant or shallow and monumental the experiences are, write them down and share with those you feel are worthy, or just keep for your self-gratification.

Launch for your brightest future. Ready, Aim, FIRE!

Remember your tears are as valuable as *Diamonds* that fall from your eyes. God catches everyone... Ps. 56:8

It is my desire that at the end of your **Diamond Journal** you can get pass... your PAST!

GOD Bless you as you get started!

# *My Diamond Journal*

**Dr. Lynda G. Washington**

*God cares about generations of curses and blessings throughout the Bible*

***Deuteronomy 7:9 KJV- Know therefore that the Lord thy God, he is God, the faithful God, which keepeth covenant and mercy with them that love him and keep his commandments to a thousand generations;***

*Note: Retiring from the public school system after approximately 30 years, being a PK, pastoring my own church, interviewing, surveying, polling, being an Elected Officials and life, I have reached these following observations. When people think you are talking about them, it is usually because they have done you wrong. This Journal is your chance to explore your experiences. Enjoy learning from what's inside YOU!*

***Ps. 139:14 Know that YOU are fearfully & wonderfully made!***

*What is your daily affirmation? What do* ***YOU*** *speak over yourself?*

________________________________________

________________________________________

________________________________________

________________________________________.

*List 5 people that influence you and why? Not celebrities please.*

________________________________________

________________________________________

________________________________________

________________________________________

________________________________________.

# My Diamond Journal

Life is a circle you prepare when you're young for your golden years... the winter years of your life. What are you doing or did you do to prepare for your golden years to take care of you? Did you follow a life plan?_____ Will you be financially stable?______

______________________________________________________________
______________________________________________________________
______________________________________________________________
______________________________________________________________
______________________________________________________________
______________________________________________________________
______________________________________________________________.

**Chapter 1-** Vada, Elena & Lynda ~ From Tears To Victories

Ladies or Gentlemen: When you begin to reflect on your last 3 generations, compare and sort the bad traits and good traits that were passed down. There are no boundaries to your mind set. Feel free to let the pin flow! Remember this is "your story", from your eyes and it might take time. You will be surprised what pops up!

Your Name ______________________________________
(Nicknames) optional

Your Mothers/Fathers Name_____________________________

Your Grandmother/Grandfather Name_____________________

Good Traits or experiences all 3 generations shared

______________________________________________________________
______________________________________________________________
______________________________________________________________.

# My Diamond Journal

Bad Traits or experiences all 3 generations shared

____________________________________________________

____________________________________________________

____________________________________________________.

List An special memory of all 3 generations that you can recall

____________________________________________________

____________________________________________________

____________________________________________________

____________________________________________________

____________________________________________________

____________________________________________________

How can you avoid the mistakes of the previous 3 generations.

____________________________________________________

____________________________________________________

____________________________________________________

How many siblings do you have? Females_______ Males ______

Have you ever been married?_________ Engaged?___________

What was the highlight of falling in love with your significant other? What went wrong....what went right.....where are you now?

____________________________________________________

____________________________________________________

____________________________________________________

____________________________________________________

____________________________________________________.

Are you willing to call a family meeting to discuss positive change?

____________________________________________________

____________________________________________________

______________________________________________

______________________________________________.

What are some of the things you can share with your next generation, to help them understand how important they are to carry on your family legacy?

______________________________________________

______________________________________________

______________________________________________.

**Chapter 2** – Daddy Don't Go

Were you raised by your biological mother? Yes No Somewhat

Were you raised by your biological father? Yes No Somewhat

Were you raised by a step or foster parent? Yes No Somewhat

Explain: The benefit or disadvantage of who raised you.

______________________________________________

______________________________________________

______________________________________________

______________________________________________.

Do you feel your childhood was a loving and nurturing one? Circle one. Yes No Somewhat Never

Explain: What do you feel could/should have been done to make your childhood more productive and safe?

______________________________________________

# My Diamond Journal

___________________________________________________________

___________________________________________________________

___________________________________________________________

___________________________________________________________.

Were there times you held your tongue from saying things to your parents that could have helped, although you had plenty to say? Yes No Sometimes Never

___________________________________________________________

___________________________________________________________

___________________________________________________________.

Were you ever left, separated or felt abandoned by a parent? Grandparent? Why what were the surrounding circumstances. Could it have possibly been prevented?

Explain:

___________________________________________________________

___________________________________________________________

___________________________________________________________

___________________________________________________________

___________________________________________________________.

Growing up did you feel you were treated differently or there was a difference in the siblings in your household?

# *My Diamond Journal*

Explain:____________________________________________

__________________________________________________

__________________________________________________

__________________________________________________

__________________________________________________

__________________________________________________.

Have you ever had someone walk out of your life? Why?

__________________________________________________.

**Chapter 3** – 2 Princesses Lynda & La Mia & 1 Prince Joseph

Oftentimes in life parents will try to make sure they treat all their children equally. My mother 100% did! Some children can make that challenging and difficult. Reflect and share some of the great things that were done to make you and your siblings feel special on a daily basis.

__________________________________________________

__________________________________________________

__________________________________________________

__________________________________________________

__________________________________________________

__________________________________________________

__________________________________________________

__________________________________________________

# My Diamond Journal

Share some of your fondness memories of Holidays! Explain in detail the preparations that were made.

# My Diamond Journal

_____________________________________________

_____________________________________________

_____________________________________________

_____________________________________________

_____________________________________________

_____________________________________________

_____________________________________________

_____________________________________________

_____________________________________________.

**Chapter 4** – God is taking over

In life we are faced with many challenges. No matter how hard you strive to raise your children right, there are people, with maybe good intentions, that can poison and introduce your child to addictions for life. Introducing them to things that are no good for them like cigarettes, cigars, alcohol, drugs, and prescription drugs, multiple sexual partners, pornography, offensiveness, lying, deceit, etc. That's not cool….at all.

It's unbelievable some of your children's friends' parents allow them to dabble in habits that you forbid. These habits can follow them for life even into adulthood. They become HOOKED and you are not even aware of it.

Name something your parents forbid you to do, that was introduced to you, by someone that you knew was wrong. Maybe you're still struggling with it til this day.

______________________________________________

______________________________________________

______________________________________________.

Are you still addicted to it today? Yes No Some Never

Did you ever tell your parents? ______ Later in life? _____

Christians practice being like Christ. **<u>Christian don't practice sin</u>**. We all may fall down, but we don't wallow in sin. We ask for God to forgive us and he does, and we **<u>STOP!</u>** Are you having a personal struggle with a habit or substance abuse you need deliverance from? Yes No

IF Yes what is it, be honest with yourself?

______________________________________________

______________________________________________.

What would it take for you to stop this habit?

____________________________________________________________

____________________________________________________________.

Do you sincerely want to be delivered?_______ why?___

Some parents allow undesirable habits for the older siblings and the younger ones are just watching, and listening. It will come up later when they get older.

Some parents <u>GIVE THEIR UNDER AGE CHILDREN LIQUOR & OTHER VISES</u> so they can monitor them...REALLY?!

Do you think it is okay to give other people children addictive substances without contacting their parents?

Explain:

____________________________________________________________

____________________________________________________________

____________________________________________________________

____________________________________________________________.

Did any of your friends' parents or older siblings ever introduce you to drugs, weed, cigarettes, liquor, or sex?

Explain:

____________________________________________________________

____________________________________________________________

# *My Diamond Journal*

______________________________________________________________

______________________________________________________________.

God wants to take over our lives. He died for us on Calvary that we could be delivered and walk in victory! When we cuss, fight, be combative and argumentative it pushes people away from us. What made your spouse, friends, co-workers love being around you, is what you need to practice staying. You were the life of every gathering. What is wrong now that friends only come around if you want to party? IF those friends won't go to church with you, that should speak volumes. You need to change your friends. Iron sharpens Iron. Are you iron?

Comments:

______________________________________________________________

______________________________________________________________

______________________________________________________________

______________________________________________________________

______________________________________________________________.

Example: IF you were a calm sweet person, even when provoked, or mad you refuse to cuss. Now you cuss for every little thing that's a turn off. If you did not smoke or drink when you first met your spouse, or friends now you drink every day, you are not viewed the same, also people say it's okay, really they don't condone it, and it makes you undesirable. When they see others that don't smoke or drink it's refreshing, and can become an actual turn on. They look forward to seeing and talking with someone that is not under the influence more than not. Who wants to be with a drunk? A substance abuser?

**Peer Pressure is real at every age!** Tell people I don't have to fit in with you. If being your friend means I have to drink, smoke, hang out in unfamiliar environments, etc. I don't need to be with you. Cutting class, having an outside affair etc. These things people do to mask the pain of life. Once you lie you have to keep lying. Beware of platonic relationships...they can be toxic and engaging as a real marriage. If your emotions run too deep you need to check that. It's intellectual intercourse, playing mind games without actual sex. There should be boundaries, when you're obsessed with someone that do not belong to you. Is that a sign or crazy in love? Ijs know your self-worth. You should desire to have your own relationship, with someone that can return your love openly and pure. Not just in your mind it's real by false acts you perceive it to be something it's clearly not.

Have you ever experienced a platonic relationship?_____

# *My Diamond Journal*

Explain:____________________________________________

___________________________________________________

___________________________________________________.

When you use substances that will end up altering your health over a period of time, you set people up around you to be prepared to take care of you, later, with serious health issues. It's fun and cool now but you are ADDICTED! Believe me from the conversations and surveys I'd polled, when that happens, it's not attractive. Although people may say its okay and laugh, they really wish you would seek counseling and **STOP!** You are setting yourself up for a heart attack or stroke then someone got to take care of you because having fun was more important than watching your health. You started with the gentle stuff now the devil has graduated you to the hard strong stuff. It takes more and more to make you feel good...you crave it and so now you are **HOOKED!**

Do you justify what you do and just play it off? Want help

Explain:

___________________________________________________

___________________________________________________

___________________________________________________

# My Diamond Journal

______________________________________________________________

______________________________________________________________.

Jesus is here to help and deliver you NOW! Let's pray.

______________________________________________________________.

They enjoy others that remind them of how you use to be. You've lost your innocence, because you're grown, and can do whatever you want? Well, someone is watching you closer than you know, especially if you have children. You will reap what you have sown. Your children are going to be just like **YOU**! God has entrusted you with so much. **GROW UP** and take responsibility be the example. An apple don't fall to far from the tree. ijs

Question: Are you willing to **STOP** bad habits to make yourself more desirable to be around and healthy?

Explain:

______________________________________________________________

______________________________________________________________

______________________________________________________________.

Why do you feel you need this crutch? Let it go today.

______________________________________________________________

______________________________________________________________

# *My Diamond Journal*

______________________________________________

______________________________________________.

A lot of people have deep hidden secrets. They live with the guilt and lies. What's really lacking that you can't handle life without substance abuse and crutches that have become habitual? Plus, it is a financial burden yearly. Add up how much you spend on recreation drugs.

Explain:

______________________________________________

______________________________________________

______________________________________________

______________________________________________.

You're spiraling, you're collapsing as others sit by watching you go downhill to bad health and damnation… First it was social, now its every day, weekends…it's serious. God will NOT dwell in an unclean temple PERIOD! We can make up all kinds of excuses, *God does NOT understand SIN and in HELL you will lift up your eyes*. Whatever it is that is keeping you from living a clean and holy life before God Almighty, is not worth your end. God is a loving God, but you will also see his wrath after being warned over and over. He knows how to get your attention and if you don't heed, mercy & grace only last for so long. Gen 6:3 God said My spirit will not strive with you always... It is God's way. Jesus paid the ultimate price for us to be delivered. Seek the Holy Spirit for strength HE is near. Aren't you tired of walking in guilt and rebellion? Pro. 14:12 There is a way that seemeth right unto a man, but the end thereof is death! It's NOT your way It's God word and His way that we must adhere to.

Explain:

______________________________________________

______________________________________________

______________________________________________

______________________________________________.

REPENT, PRAY & GET DELIVERED today..... Find someone you trust to pray with you. The devil is the accuser of the brethren. Jesus intervenes for us. He is here to help you.

WARNING ***Some people will actually not stop until they pull you in sin with them! Sexual, smoking, drinking, plotting fornication, adultery, idolatry, hypocrisy, lies etc. ***They want you dirty like them***. It makes them feel better. Your righteousness they hate. They think they hate you, but it's the God in your life that judges them every time they see you. Therefore, you are not a welcome visitor, but God sees, hears and knows all that is whispered and all deeds done in the dark will surface.

IF you choose to live riotous, continuously sin and be hell bound, go by yourself. Don't keep pulling and trying to convince and to corrupt others that are trying to live free from sin, because you want to be dirty and nasty.

John 3:19 men loved darkness rather than light, because their deeds were evil.

Gossipers and feet that run to spread confusion God hates. Matt. 22: 36-40 We must LOVE the Lord our God with all our heart...You are commissioned to love your neighbor as yourself. People don't have love for each other no more like they use to. Everyone is short tempered, quick to count you out. Drop you like a bad habit and don't look back but we say we are Christians.

God does not tolerate sin in NONE OF US! No one is exempt, the Preacher, the Sunday School teacher, The church mother or members. We **MUST LOVE** and **FORGIVE** everyone including your boss, co-workers, neighbors, family, ex's, back biters, haters, and those that plot again you etc. with the I John 4:7-8 Agape love of Christ. THERE IS NO OTHER WAY! I John 2:15 – Love not the world….

Comments:

______________________________________________

______________________________________________

______________________________________________.

**Chapter 5** – A storybook wedding….. Kenny & Lynda

Pro. 18:22 Whosoever findeth a wife findeth a good thing…LOVE is a many splendor thing! Everyone wants to be happy, fulfilled, desired, wanted, cry, live and share special moments with someone they want to be with.

Who is the person that tickles your insides? ___________

Who do you enjoy that lights up your day? ___________

Have you ever been in love?______ Unconditional? ____

How many times?_______ Puppy______ REAL ________

How did you meet that special someone? How did it make you feel to hear their name? See their face? Aaww

Explain:

______________________________________________

______________________________________________

# *My Diamond Journal*

______________________________________________________________

_____________________________________________________________.

A true lover is someone that is truthful, honest, loving, passionate, providing, <u>sacrificing</u>, sees your faults and covers you, protects you, while praying with you etc. Their words are soothing. They stand firm with you.

What are some of the qualities that make him/her so special to you?

______________________________________________________________

______________________________________________________________

_____________________________________________________________.

A narcissist is someone that dreams and lies about **everything**, period! They are admirers of themselves and <u>totally selfish</u>. There is no proof of anything they pretend to have. They are great actors full of deceit, very hurtful.

What are some of the things looking back on now, that you know are/were red flags, and you should have keep it moving for real! They were so convincing and you believed them after they said "You can trust me baby".

Pathological liars are hard to discern, crafty with words.

Are you looking for beauty or intergrity?______ Why?___

# *My Diamond Journal*

______________________________________________

______________________________________________

______________________________________________.

**Chapter 6** – Everyone is gone?! My grandkids!

**Empty Nest Syndrome** is real! When everyone is gone & there is no more pitter patter of feet running through the house, and no more family noise in the home, you can feel lonely, slip into a depression and rejection, and it hurts. Having a miscarriage can cause Empty Nest Syndrome and your arms will actually hurt to hold a baby. Feel like the walls are closing in on you all around.

But God made some cute, cuddly, getting into everything little people called "Grandkids"! OMG! Don't you love those grandparents that wear your ears off about how adorable and smart their grandkids are with 100 pics?

What is it about your grandkids or someone with grandkids you know, that just keep a "big grin" on your face! They know how to look at you until you say YES!

Comment:

______________________________________________

______________________________________________

______________________________________________

# My Diamond Journal

________________________________________________

________________________________________________.

Jesus said except we be like little children we cannot enter into the kingdom. Matt. 19:14 Suffer the little children …. We don't have to teach children certain behaviors. Some they learn from watching and listening to us. Some of their behavior and mood is second nature.

A true story: My oldest grandson Lil K. J. when he was 9 was selected to participate in a Spelling Bee and he won and moved on to the next level. He was winning at the regional level, spelling the words correctly, and he would look back at me and smile every time he stood, received his word, spelled it correctly and sat down, waiting for his next word. I promise they gave other children words like bank, suit, table etc. they gave my grandson words like hamster, violin, refrigerator etc. Then they gave him the word borrow. He spelled it with one r and he was told "that's incorrect" and to sit down. It was incorrect and he fell embarrassed, shame, and disappointment. He never looked back at me. He just kept his head forward and I could see the tears dropping from his eyes. I was torn and wanted to go get him, and take him out, but he had to sit through it until it was over. The fact that when he didn't perform well he felt hurt, and wouldn't make eye contact with me, just that emotion was beyond overwhelming for me, and him. Of course his parents and I took him out to dinner and celebrated him making it almost to the end. That was a valuable lesson for me that no one taught him, feel hurt and be ashamed, when you miss the mark. It was a natural emotion within him at 9?

But we taught him how to handle it saying by cheering him on with praise. Telling him, Next year you'll be back and you'll knock it out! He was smiling and felt better because of our support. His self- esteem was back on point, with just a little encouragement. What I'm saying is we all need to be like little children and stop pretending things don't bother us, when it's literally tearing us apart inside. Be truthful with yourself, and use it as a stepping stone to keep moving to the next round. My grandson is a straight A student and excel in every area academically. He and his brothers are 3 grades level above grade average at the least. I thank God for that experience. WOW! I learned more than he did that day.

All 4 of my grandchildren are very territorial with me, and vis versa. We are complete when we are together and we don't like to share each other. They LOVE me and

I LOVE them. We genuinely never tire of hanging out together! Whenever we get together it's all good!

Have you ever felt embarrassed or hurt about something and people knew it? What was it? What did you learn?

Explain:________________________________________

______________________________________________

______________________________________________

______________________________________________.

## Chapter 7 – Politricks & Face book Over kill

As an Elected Official I learned about the real dirty and conniving tricks people play. From my observation, I made up the word Politricks! In 2013 I ran against 17 people and I won a Trustee seat in Sauk Village, IL. I was the only one that was not an incumbent that won, with Gods help. Then I ran for Mayor of Sauk Village, IL. 2017, I lost my race. I fought a good hard persistent fight with my team of supporters and sponsors. There were females that did not vote for me, just because they did not want me to go down in history as the first woman Mayor of Sauk Village, IL. They did not want to be the Mayor, and didn't even serve on any community committees, but just wanted to be spiteful and not vote for me. Although I was working hard, implementing many successful programs through my Neighborhood Watch Program making history with signs throughout the Village, inclusive of plays, concerts, videos etc. My opponents worked hard against me. They plotted and paid youth and police allegedly to pull up my yard signs and throw away my literature in businesses and homes. This was told to me. My enemies teamed up together. Then by the end of the election they had all turned on each other. I still feel like a winner because I did my best.

Warning: **Did you know that...People that do not like each other, will come together to sabotage your dream**? They honestly cannot stand each other but they will stand together to make sure you fail. Then they go back to not liking each other after they are sure your dream is dead! Even on your job people will set you up, lie, spy, keep confusion going on but in the end, they come to no good finish. Hurting people hurt people. I have truly discovered. Friends can quickly become your enemies.

In my work history of 45 years from various places of employment, I had 3 of the worst bosses you could ever imagine. In the beginning they were all kind, professional and fair. After people saw the working relationship we had, they begin to tell my boss things about me that were simply lies. They were determined to get me fired and written up by starting a paper trail, for trivial and frivolous purposes. Daily, for years, I was picked on, abused, used, made to do degrading things to humiliate me in front of my peers and co-workers. The ones that was behind this attacks, encouraging my bosses would laugh to see me enduring so much hateful, negative and intentional ridicule daily. They got a good laugh about it.

God will fight your battles. If you keep still and continue to pray. Some of them had accidents, was transferred, fired and passed away. Just hateful and full of the fact they could assert their authority any way they pleased, they thought. Although they had the ear of man, I had the ear of God. I KNOW FOR MYSELF THAT GOD WILL HANDLE PEOPLE THAT TRY TO DESTROY HIS CHILDREN!

Matt. 18:1-6 It is better for him that a millstone were hanged about his neck.....Don't bother children of God.

The political world is very unpredictable. People smile in your face and turn and make a phone call and sell you for 30 pieces of silver like Judas did Jesus. After spending thousands of dollars and people promising you that you can depend on them. I promise you they will walk away and not look back! People will leave you out there to figure it out all **by yourself**. You better know God got your back and he will NEVER leave or forsake you. It was an experience. My political aspirations have only just begun. It ani't over yet! Amen! God is still writing my life!

What politicians have influenced your life? Do you VOTE?! Are you involved in your local government?_____

Explain:________________________________________

________________________________________________

________________________________________________

_______________________________________________.

Face Book is the new hate pool to laundry your feelings and make certain people feel left out. Doesn't it amaze you how some people LIKE and COMMENT everything some people write, and they never LIKE or make a COMMENT about anything you post no matter how good? They know you watching these people I delete.

Have anyone ever done this to you? Offended you on fb.

________________________________________________

________________________________________________

________________________________________________

_______________________________________________.

Face Book can be very offensive. Family will Unfriend you, tag each other, leave you out the loop. Acknowledge certain family members birthdays, graduation, pics etc. They won't compliment or say nothing on your page smhh. They never call you or say I'm proud of you…ever.

When people show you who they are BELIEVE THEM!!!

Have you experienced this childish type of offense on fb?

______________________________________________

______________________________________________

______________________________________________

______________________________________________.

**Chapter 8**- The KEL-LAW Foundation, Inc. (The L.A.W!)

I Co-Founded a Non for Profit Organization with years of successful programs for over 25 years with a 501c3! We served Chicagoland area and the South Suburbs. Now I have my own Non for Profit Organization The **Dr. Lynda G. Washington Foundation**! We have applied for our 501c3 as well. My ministry **J.I.L.O.T.A. Worldwide Ministries, Inc**. have applied for our 501c3 as well. God is blessing us with a double 501c3 access, to bless the community. I also made up an inspirational line dance for events call **The L.A.W!** Love Always Wins! I teach it for parties, events and weddings. We preform it, you can view it on Youtube! Type in my name Lynda Washington ...Enjoy! I have the greatest Board Of Directors in the world! Volunteers are faithful, dependable and focused.

Have you started or been a part of an Organization?____

______________________________________________

______________________________________________

______________________________________________.

**Chapter 9**- Miracles Personified

Ex. 15:26 ...I am the Lord your healer. God is still working Miracles for them that believe! He is a Healer, Provider, Comforter, Lawyer, Doctor, way maker, etc. I know there are things that have happened in your life and you couldn't believe it. Maybe you felt like Man how did that happen? God loves us and desires to give us the keys to the kingdom. No good thing will he withhold from them that love him. Don't you trust God with your health? ___

Do you believe in Miracles? _____ Do you pray?_____

Can you name at least 3 Miracles you have received?

# *My Diamond Journal*

____________________________________________

____________________________________________

____________________________________________

____________________________________________.

**Chapter 10-** Who don't love Jesus?

This is a mean cruel world. Violence is prevalent on every hand. There is senseless killings, shootings and murders toward all ages, sex, gender, races and in general. The youth and seniors are not the only targets. They are performing mass murders in school, churches, concerts, and clubs also on open highways. I know Jesus is in charge but you have to invite him in. They kicked prayer out the schools. So Jesus left out and the devil is taking over some believe. I wouldn't want to know life without God. We must pray as a community, family, and nation.

Would you like to see prayer back in the schools? _____

Do you pray with your family before you leave daily? ___

Is a thankful prayer said by your family at night? ______

IF you could make the decision to cooperate Jesus back into our society, what steps would you take?

Explain:

______________________________________________

______________________________________________

______________________________________________

______________________________________________.

**Chapter 11** – When In Laws Become Out Laws

The IN LAWS from HELL!!! Lock the doors, turn off the lights act like we're not home! Above all don't answer the phone! Maybe they will leave if we throw hints! LOL

Well this is a broad subject, that usually starts verbal and physical fights, brawls even. Well, let's start by saying it is a common belief that the girls family always gets first choice. Her people name the baby. What the boy's people want to name the baby, isn't even considered. The grandchildren are always at the girl's parent's house. The boys' parents are always a last resort. The girls' parents are praised for the simplest gifts. The boys' parents can buy monumental gifts and they are barely recognized. The girls' parents are often asked for advice regarding child rearing while the boys' parents simply aren't involved unless they happen to hear about an incident. Then their consider to be nosey or meddling. The girl sometimes recent her husband relationship with his mother, wish is just plain ignorant. The girl calls her dad for things all the time, and sees no reason why her husband should feel threaten. These are call DOUBLE STANDARDS! Most real women go beyond, to be close to their mother in law, it makes their husband happy. NO REAL MAN WANT TO DEAL WITH HIS WIFE AND MOTHER AT ODDS. He knows deep inside they recent each other because they both complain to him! Poor Man always in the middle found trying to please both. There is no choice. They both have their special place. The Bible says leave all and cleave to your mate Gen. 2:24. Reality the divorce rate is so high there may be a divorce, and you will no longer be their mate. But his/her parents won't change. I have a friend that told her daughter in law in arguing, when her daughter In law told her I got him wrapped! He ani't going no where! I can do for him something you can't do! And his mom simply replied, "One day you might not be his wife, but I will always be his mother"! Some daughter in laws choose to fight against their mother in law, once they get the man. Before the marriage they're really engaging with his family, visiting, calling, sharing and just so sweet. But, after they get them they won't even answer your phone call, you are the last person they want to be around and when his family come around they quickly excuse themselves or stay on their phone like they're so busy. Yes, truly he is the only common thread between you … Boys are not that common with their mother in laws to call them all day and discuss issues, they are just respectful …… and that's normal. You can't compare it..ijs

There are test in all walks of life even for Christians.

Do you have a good engaging real relationship with your:

Mother In Law _____ Why?________________________

Father In Law _____ Why? ________________________

Sister In Law ______ Why?_________________________

Brother In Law _____ Why? ________________________

What would it take to make these relationships better?

_______________________________________________

_______________________________________________

_______________________________________________.

What went wrong?_______________________________

Have you considered sitting down having a one on one?

_______________________________________________

# *My Diamond Journal*

IF Jesus comes back or you pass will this keep you out of heaven?________________________________________

They killed Jesus and He prayed and died for them still.

Everyone in the families are watching, show God's love.

Can you stand before God in pure innocence? __________

Do you believe the 10 commandments? ______________

It's hard to preach what you don't live as a Christian. Ijs

You know people that attend Church on Sundays and still full of hate, bitterness, mean, rude, temperamental …WOW! Hey, you better not tell them they not going to heaven. Don't God understand they have a reason to hate and not show 100% agape love. They special…The bible says you're like a sounding brass when you pray!

Note: It's easier to love than to have contention, if there is conflict, for Christ sake get over it, life is too short, repent and show the love as Christ would. Some situations are irreparable, too much has been said and done. You forgave some but not all. Is that your current situation? Some you can easily forgive for all they have said that was very offensive. Others you hold grudges toward and never try to repair or restore that precious relationship. You're stuck in the pass. What a sad waste.

Explain: ______________________________________________

______________________________________________

______________________________________________

______________________________________________

Then again, most can be worked out so family visits can be pleasant for all, it will make your mate happy when they see true love and affection shown between the ones he/she loves. I'm sure there is more good things than bad. Think about the good times, just start being kind.

**Chapter 12** – Metamorphism of pain…I made your Glory

Metamorphism is a change in form. Some people set out to purposely build you up to let you down. In some families siblings struggle with favoritism. Its believed that certain children are the parents favorite. Some parent will get in their children's faces, young or grown, and reduce them to tears by degrading them. Calling them hurtful names. Saying things like "I wish I never had you!"

Some people are possessed with a manipulative and witchcraft spirit. Dominating is their thrill at any cost. The more you sacrifice the more they expect you to do, and when you don't, they turn against you in a most destructive way. Usually emotionally, I've seen people strive to please family members at any cost. Any little thing they can do to keep them happy and loving them they are willing to do. These same people are so short patient with everybody else. Could they be bipolar?____

Do you know people that get a thrill out of hurting you?

______________________________________________

Do you get emotional if certain family members ignore you? ________________________________________

Can you say you feel you are the black sheep?__________

______________________________________________

Are you tired of being: left out?________ Involved? ______

Do you often feel shut out or not in the family loop? _____

Do people owe you money and stay away? ____________

Do you feel lonely or happy at family gatherings? Why?

Explain:______________________________________

______________________________________________

______________________________________________

______________________________________________.

# *My Diamond Journal*

**I Made Your Glory** – Build A Family!   Start from scratch!

Do you know there are thousands of people that feel rejection just like you? You can actually reach out to others and have a fulfilling life. If you have family members that don't want, or appreciate you, BUILD A FAMILY! Get with people like you and make a family.

I have God daughters, God sons, spiritual daughters and sons. I have work daughters and sons. My life is full of people that want me in their lives. It's too many people that want a mother, father, grandmother, grandfather, son, daughter figure in their daily lives. Get involved with people that celebrate YOU! You have a lot to give and a winning personality. STOP wishing you had love get in where you fit in. Get a hobby, change your circle, make new friends that are worthy of your input. They are waiting to meet YOU! Start today don't be afraid to love.

Out with the old way of thinking In with the NEW thinking! Celebrate and be happy EVERYDAY! Smile!

Are you willing to try meeting new friends?________

Where will you start?_____________________________

**Be encouraged and don't apologize if people want in your life, where others disregard you. LIVE in PEACE!**

**Chapter 13** – Pastor/Evangelist E. R. Allen-Staten

Pastor E. R. Allen-Staten the Founder of Christ Bible Center located at 134 E. 111thStreet, in the Roseland Area of Chicago, IL. Was a great Woman of God. She was noted as The Hardest Working Evangelist, because we had church Thursday, Friday, Saturday, Sunday Morning and Sunday Night Television Broadcast every week. It was packed with full deliverance services. When people feel the Spirit of God they like to stay around and just fellowship. She never put people out the church after services. Oftentimes up 4 hours later, we all still would be just there sharing, musician playing and we singing and talking enjoying Christian fellowship. She believed God house should be open to serve more than a weekly bible class and 1 hour service on Sunday. Religion and a format was not the norm for our church. We let the Holy Spirit have his way. People are hurting and the demand for deliverance is great. Churches should be open every day like a spiritual hospital, especially in this day and time with so much evil and violence. We showed gospel movies, had gospel based activities for the saints of all ages. She was an Educator for the Board of Ed. She was a powerful spiritual leader in the Community with a great Television Ministry. She sacrificed her life literally to preach the gospel and to win souls at any cost. She was known as a love vessel. She LOVED people that despiteful used her, and took her kindness for weakness, even some family members. You ever had some family members treat you poorly and all you did was love, provided and covered them? Some never returned the love she seeked. On the other hand, hundreds of thousands loved her tremendously, and showed it with great appreciation. Sometimes, it's not the one's you do the most for. Believe me, your love and respect will come from those you did the least for. That's no blood kin to you. She prided herself by representing The African American race with dignity and excellence. She saw other races on T. V. and she did represent with high quality on every level for God's glory! Her personal life could not compare to her spiritual life and gratification. She loved Jesus and had the heart of everyone she came in contact with of all races and religions. She was extremely intelligent and excelled highly in everything she did. God blessed her. Thousands are in ministry all over the four corners of the world today, that came through her church and ministry. The testimonies are endless even over 23 years after her death. What a legacy! THINK! What will your legacy be? Are we working to build one?

# *My Diamond Journal*

Explain:____________________________________________

__________________________________________________

__________________________________________________

__________________________________________________

__________________________________________________.

She pioneered the way for many women Pastors. She was on Television, Radio and traveled extensively, preaching the Word of God. Thousands of great and miraculous documented Miracles followed her ministry.

I want to challenge your spiritual walk in Christ. When you leave this earth what will people remember you for?

__________________________________________________

__________________________________________________.

How many years have you been saved? ______

How many years have you been delivered?_______

Are you baptized? ________ Are your children? ________

How many years have you been born again?__________

How many years have you been a Christian? __________

How many souls/people have you invited to church this:

Week?_________ Month?_______ Year?____ Ever?____

How many of your friends know you are a Christian? ___

# *My Diamond Journal*

Do you pray at restaurants over your food? __________

How many hours a week do you spend Witnessing?____

Prayer ____ Bible Reading ____ Church____ Other_____

Do you call and encourage someone you know need it?_

Can you be considered a Prayer Warrior? ________

Do you talk about Jesus to anyone?____ Anywhere?____

Do you play gospel music or the bible at home? ______

How is your church attendance?________ Tithing? _____

Is there anything in your home that when friends come over they will know this is a Christian home? _________

Note: Some Christian have ash trays, or wine available for smokers, some have alcohol in their refrigerator, packs of cigarettes and weed for casual recreation they say. Using the money blessed you with health and strength to make to purchase sinful pleasures. This hurts the heart of God. Everything we do is being recorded. We will give an account of it when we stand before God. It doesn't matter if you believe it or not. The bible says: Romans 14:11 and Phil. 2:11 EVERY knee shall bow and EVERY tongue shall confess that Jesus Christ is Lord... WE will all truly stand before God and be accountable. Don't let the devil make you think God loves you more than HE does his only begotten son Jesus. If he turned his back on him when he became sin on the cross, and he had to do that, to redeem us, he will surely send you to hell if **you choose the things and lust of your flesh.** Are our habits worth us missing heaven? ______ Deut. 30:15 & 19. **This day I call the heavens and the earth as witnesses against you that I have set before you life and death, blessings and curses. Now choose life, so that *<u>you and your children may live.</u>* God does not understand SIN!**

Are you willing to start today winning souls for Christ?__

Anyone that is NOT saved is LOST, it's just that simple.

Repent, Pray and move forward. Take someone to church with you. Invite families in your neighborhood or have a community bible class in your back yard once a month. It's time to make big changes for Gods Kingdom!

What are you doing to get souls aware of the seriousness of making a decision to follow Christ? How many of your "friends" are Christians? _______ Be specific birds of a feather flock together, so they say. Who are your friends? Do they attend church anywhere? Really….

Explain:

______________________________________________________________

______________________________________________________________

______________________________________________________________

______________________________________________________________.

**Chapter 14** – Where The Christians AT? Where Are **YOU**?

**WAKE UP CHRISTIANS! JESUS IS COMING BACK SOON!**

I Thess. 4:17 Then we which are alive and remain shall be "caught up" together with the Lord….. I am going up!

I have heard saints that walk with God that proclaim to be saved say " I hope I go up", "It's up to God who he takes", "I'm not gonna say that cause …." Well, I want to take a pause right here to let you know; that I know, that I know, without a shadow of a doubt, when Jesus returns for His church, I am going up in the Rapture with Him!

You can have whatsoever you say…you can be unsure.

As for me and my house we are going back with Jesus!

Jesus is going to **Rapture** his church! Will you be ready?

Let's get in the street and have revival. Churches are closed more than they are open. If your church is always collecting money and not on t.v. or radio and have no outreach ministry what are you collecting money for? Just to have a big bank account? No feeding program, not building a new church or have been having a building fund for over 10 years and still do not have the church yet? Let's get serious about God's will and hit the streets. Everyone is not going to come to church. Go where they are and minister. God is not limited to move inside a church only. PREACH God's word everywhere he will lead

Luke 14:23 – Go out into the highways and hedges and compel them to come in that my house may be filled.... God told us to go and reach the lost. Where are the Christians At?! I never see saints out passing out tracks no more do you? Knocking on doors, inviting people to come to your church. Some pastors are content with having the same members, and have no outreach in place so the church can grow! Every church should be out at the malls, bus stations, game, community events, etc. passing out tracks to win souls for Christ. So many people are on drugs, alcohol etc. because they have no hope. Where the Christians At? We must increase our plea and pray with families. If you don't know how go to your pastor. Some saints been in church 10, 20, 30 years just sitting and doing nothing to grow the Kingdom of

God. We are his disciples that have the answer. What are you waiting on to witness for the Lord? How much longer

Explain:________________________________________

________________________________________

________________________________________.

Now the Bible is on the smart phone and computers with an app. Saints do not carry their Bible anymore and satan loves that! He does not want to see it, and he does not want anyone else to see it. Children don't have a bible and some have never attended Sunday School to learn about God. Every child should have a bible and a time to read it, and be taught the things he desires of us. When was the last time you took your family to a Christian book store, and brought books for everyone? I still carry my physical bible in public. Even when I was in high school I carried it. I wanted to. The way Christ was presented to me, I wanted everyone to know I am a follower of Christ. I even go to the public library so people can see, I'm not ashame of Jesus Christ. Will you?

How do you feel about saints not carrying their bibles in public, even to church no more? Are you will to try it?

# *My Diamond Journal*

______________________________________________

______________________________________________

______________________________________________.

It's okay to have apps of the Bible, but always know nothing substitutes you standing up boldly, for Christ by carrying your Bible in public. You don't have to say a word when people see it there is still conviction and remembrance about God, church and wholesome living.

Would you carry your Bible to work? ____ Try it for a week. See the response you will get. Take it anywhere.

This generation do not know about some of the following Christian attributes that make us strong as a unit. The adults have dropped the ball and simply do not want to be bothered, with other people children to teach them. Adults of today will volunteer to do everything on all kinds of charitable and community outreach, but we are failing the youth of today. MAKE TIME TO MENTOR! The next generation needs your knowledge, please make the sacrifice and save a life, save a soul, save our world!

Where are the Christians At that use to be outside on the corners & downtown passing out tracks? Will you go?

# *My Diamond Journal*

______________________________________________

______________________________________________.

Where are the Christians At that had Shut-Ins? All night.

______________________________________________

______________________________________________.

Where are the Christians At that called a church fast?

______________________________________________

______________________________________________.

Where are the Christians At that minister in the jails, nursing homes, hospitals, visit the sick at home, call the backsliders that been missing church, passing out bibles?

______________________________________________

______________________________________________.

Would you wear a Christian buttons, T-shirts, jackets?

______________________________________________.

Where are the Christians At to take the youth gospel skating, bowling, picnics, and other fun gospel centered activities? We are failing the next generation **WAKE UP**!

______________________________________________

______________________________________________.

# *My Diamond Journal*

Where are the Christians At with Gospel Concerts more than on Mother's Day? We need more Christian Events.

______________________________________________

______________________________________________.

Where are the women ~ get the girls for Christ groups?

______________________________________________

Where are the men ~ get the boys for Christ groups?

______________________________________________

______________________________________________

When was the last time you went to Sunday school?

______________________________________________

Are your children aware and train in the ways of Christ?

______________________________________________.

What will you say when you see **Jesus** face to face?

Jesus is coming soon. The rapture is about to take place any minute. We as Christians should be focused on one thing as a Church and that's SOUL WINNING! Not joining a church but joining the family of God by accepting Jesus Christ as your personal savior. If we don't tell them their blood will be on your hands in the judgement day. Remember ANYONE you know that is not saved is hell bound. It is our Christian responsibility to introduce our family, friends, co-workers, neighbors and associates to Christ. Some will accept some won't but you must share.

That's what we as Christians are commissioned to do. Your friends are going to hate you if they go to hell, a place where they will NEVER get out! You better tell the story of HIS glory to everyone you see, and talk to start NOW! The devil will tell you "They don't want to hear that"! He wants them to go to hell, but give them that option. Witness for HIM so he will stand up for YOU!

**Chapter 15** – J.I.L.O.T.A. Worldwide Ministries, Inc.

Jesus Is Lord Of This Army Worldwide Ministries, Inc. focuses on saving the lost at any cost. We are a group of believers from various denominations, walks of life, believers that are not ashamed and **BOLDLY witness for Jesus Christ** anywhere and anytime without hesitation. This is the church I pastored over 4 years that was named by my mother the last Pastor E. R. Allen- Staten in 1995.

IF you are not a soul winner and you want to learn how to witness effectively for the Lord, we are the group you want to be with! This world is mean and evil but our God is greater and mightier than any one. He is God Almighty!

We specialize in witnessing one on one or in groups. Our street ministry is constant and growing. You are welcome to come and participate. I encourage you to go on my web page jilota4law.com for updates. Don't ever hesitate to tell your neighbors and friends about God. You might be the last opportunity they have to turn their life around. If you are not ashame to let the world know you are a Christian I challenge you again to get your Bible and begin to pass out tracks for the Lord. DO NOT GO ALONE!

Talk to your pastor and see IF they have a group you can go with. IF not ask him/her can you start a group to help build the congregation. It should be no problem at all.

**Chapter 16** – Are you stuck? Are you a **dreamer** or **visionary**?

Sometimes in life you know what you want to achieve but looks like the goal is so far off and it takes a lot of money, planning and energy. If you are not motivated time will pass by. Before you know it time flies by and your dream is still just a wish. If people treat time like money they wouldn't waste it. Time waits for no one, minutes turn to days, days turn to weeks, weeks turn to months and months turn to years! Another year gone by and nothing is achieved. You must set yourself short and long term goals.

Are you a **dreamer** (a wisher procrastinator excuses) It's never the right time for any reason...but I'm claiming it!

Explain:

________________________________________________

________________________________________________

________________________________________________

________________________________________________.

Are you a **visionary** (make it happen against all odds refuse to wait) I don't know how but I'm starting NOW!

Explain:

________________________________________________

________________________________________________

________________________________________________

________________________________________________.

**Chapter 17** – World wind of Praises then Hallelujah Anyhow!

Remember, we don't walk by sight but by Faith in God! Things will go wrong and life is full of disappointments, but praise God anyway. God is the reason for all my success. He leads and guides me and shows me my path.

Having a relationship with God is the most real and profound thing I do on a daily basis. Praying and interceding for my family is my priority. I give all the praises to God for great things he is continually doing in my life. I claim the FAVOR of God in all things I do. Amen!

Do you ever feel overwhelmed and hard to praise God?

______________________________________________

______________________________________________.

What do you feel different when you pray concerning it?

______________________________________________

______________________________________________.

Can you praise God in good and hard times? __________

Smile, laugh out loud, literally throw your head back and embrace your new destiny today. You’re on your way!

How do you release all the cares and stress of this world?

______________________________________________

______________________________________________.

You should feel happier already, just let it go. God said cast your cares on him for his yoke is easy and his burdens are light. Ps. 55:22 Cast thy burdens upon the LORD, and he shall sustain thee… Jesus will blow your mind. Talk to him he will answer and you will be free.

Don't let nobody remove you off your standards ever.

Follow your heart it won't mislead you, trust you.

***Final Thoughts***: Did you Get pass your PAST?! I sincerely hope you have released some emotions you had kept locked inside. As you read through your **"Diamond Journal" work on yourself.** Compare your answers.

After I lost my race for Mayor God blessed me with My T.V. Show entitled: **The RE-YOU Show!** You can see it on Youtube! If you don't like your life **RE-YOU** yourself. Do you over, don't stay there. Everyone loves the concept and the popularity is spreading all glory be to God. We are viewed in 90 countries! God is a miracle worker and great business man. The world is waiting on you. Don't settle this time. Wait on God, it will be better and you're worth the wait. It is not important to change the world. Some people missed their biggest blessing by leaving you. God will give you double for all your loss. Just wait Ps. 30:5 says Weeping may endure for a night but joy cometh in the morning! It's morning whenever you wake up! So wake up no matter what time it is on the clock! It's a mental state of mind, you must believe it's your time! My theme for 2018 is: ***I'M WALKING IN MY NOW***! My wait is over ***NOW! I don't have to wait no more!!!***

Save yourself, some people won't go to your next chapter with you. Yes, know you might have to cry sometimes, but I promise you Jesus, is right there in it with you. I know it's been unbearable at times, but you are not alone. Millions suffer in silence but that's no longer your story. Your future is bright and filled with precious and mind blowing surprises. Happiness has arrived. You should be skipping in your heart, it's real.

There are some things you can tell people and they don't want to hear it from you... They need the information you have but they don't want you to be the one to tell them. But, LIFE, will teach you some things. Life is a journey and everything they don't want to hear from you, when LIFE teach it to them, they will wish they would have just listened. That smart mouth is quiet down. Just pray and watch God bring it to past. YES!

Some people will listen and they avoid hardship and years of wasting time going in circles just to prove you wrong. So senseless when you see people marching in place in life. They become stagnated, cease developing become inactive or dull, instead of moving forward, they get defensive when you try to encourage them to make moves, make changes, they really get aggravated with you. You're annoying because you're trying to get them out their rut and GROW! Now... Are you ready? Stand up and shake off that old weary person! Only you can make it happen. Just make a little effort. God will do the rest.

Well, get excited this is your new beginning! Speak positive things over yourself. Mark 11:24 You can have whatsoever YOU say. So start saying some creative things over your situations. Look with expectancy for positive channels. Hang around positive people that trust you.

Change your circle see the difference. Real friends never leave. You talk it out and reconcile. If people leave you let them go! I have my Master's Degree in saying Good Bye! It's a changing of the guards! Some people just are not good for you and they don't know why they behave the way they do. So just exhale and know God is in control. You can live without anyone but God! Amen!

# *My Diamond Journal*

Anything that leaves your life, God will replace it with someone or something better. Let your positive demeanor be contagious to all around you. Amen!

I'm a living witness IF you be faithful and hold on and let God make the choice, you will experience unbelievable happiness. YES…. ***"He'll Turn Your Tears To Diamonds"!***

Winning Souls For Christ,

Dr. Lynda G. Washington

Author & Evangelist

***For Booking Engagements & Book Tour Request:***


Dr. Lynda G. Washington

P. O. Box 1671

Sauk Village, IL. 60412

For more information call (708) 359-2746

Email: jilotawwm@yahoo.com

Web Page: jilota4law.com


Follow me on Face Book, Twitter, Instagram, LinkedIN, Marco Polo and more! We would love to come teach your group our line dance The LAW!

www.ingramcontent.com/pod-product-compliance
Lightning Source LLC
LaVergne TN
LVHW081423110826
845149LV00010B/1849
*9780990934868*